In the name of Allah, the Lord of the macrocosm

Musharraf Shaheen

The Srinagar Smart City

Presented to...............................

From..

Musharraf Shaheen

The Srinagar Smart City

Propositions and Recommendations

Musharraf Shaheen

The Majestic Penn®

fostering creativity

ISBN-10:1545245401
ISBN-13:978-1545245408

The Srinagar Smart City

"Peace and Tranquility are the staple and cardinal *sine qua nons* for Sustainable Development."

Musharraf Shaheen

DEDICATION

*This Booklet is dedicated to my beloved Grandma
Late Khadija Mir and my adorable maternal
Grandpa Late Wali Muhammad Turi.*

CONTENTS

PROLOGUE

Smart City can be elucidated as " A city reaping the benefits of *a la mode* equipments, bereft of savagery and an ideally ideal nerve centre for erudition, education and knowledge." A sans blemish Smart wen is brought into being by Sustainable Development which perchance is the most solicitous bone of contention in third world countries.

This opus was initially written for an Essay Competition orchestrated by Srinagar Municipal Corporation in 2016 but lucklessly it didn't end up at the superscripted point of disembarkation in view of enervated postal services in the Vale due to curfewed days and nights.

"While inscribing on the paper this opus, a myriad of peeps quenched and dampened me down but I had the courage and valor like that of Grand mortals which prompted me to ecrire this opus."

Musharraf Shaheen

INTRODUCTION

If one were to praise Kashmir, whole books would have been written. Kashmir is a garden of eternal spring, or an iron fort to a palace of Kings —a delightful flower-bed, and a heart expanding heritage for dervishes. Its pleasant meads and enchanting cascades are beyond all description. There are running streams and fountains beyond count. Wherever the eye reaches, there is verdure and running water. The red rose, the violet and the narcissus grow of themselves in the fields, there are all kinds of flowers and all sorts of sweet-scented herbs, more than can be calculated. In the soul enchanting spring, the hills and plains are filled with blossoms; the gates, the walls, the courts, the roofs are lighted up by the torches of the banquet-adoring tulips.

While breathing the words of splendor, beauty, grandeur and glamour of the nanoscopic facsimile of Eden, it is injustice and villainy not to reveal the artistry and grandeur of its heart i.e.; Srinagar.

Srinagar- the summer capital and the premier wen of the vale has its idiosyncratic and cultural, historical and religious rarity. The gorgeousness and pulchritude of the city has procured renown, stardom and fame in the entire orb. The world venerable and famous tourist sites viz Dal Lake, Nishat, Shalimar, Chesma Shahi, Pari Mahal, Harwan and Nagin Lake are the feathers gleaming and glistening on its cap. From religious panorama, Srinagar is realm to world venerable religious sites like Khanqah-e-Moula, Jamia Masjid, Hazaratbal Shrine, Makhdoom Sahib, Dastgeer Sahib, Shankar Achariya and Chhatti Padshahi Gurudwara. In short, a vacation to this heart of the paradise, resplendent in nature's glory, will linger long in the memory of the visitant.

GOALS FOR THE CITY

1. Cleanest and the most tranquil, serene and harmonious burgh on the sphere.

   2. Par excellence drainage system supplemented with *a la mode* technology.

   3. A conurbation sans penury, pauperdom and poverty.

4. Nanoscopic swatch towns to be initiated like that of *Choki Dani* in Rajasthan to spectacle and array the splendor, grandeur, artistry, culture and heritage of *the Eden*.

5. Museums and Libraries should be developed to initiate the penchant and predilection for poetry, History and other literary works related to the Vale.

6. Development and instigation of adventurous and venturesome sports viz Trekking and Swimming etc.

7. Development of Royal Springs Golf Course and S.K Cricket Stadium with unique and idiosyncratic world class

provisions and facilities.

8. Libraries should be instigated and developed on the banks of Dal Lake.

9. Public insight into the above propounded goals and *raisons d'être* and the *will to do* and perpetrate the plan of action for ideal and archetypal Smart City.

The Srinagar Smart City

THE PECULIARITIES OF THE
WEN

Srinagar-the premier burgh of the nanoscopic facsimile of Eden is cradle to *sui generis* Kashmiri culture and heritage. From mellifluous and dulcet Kashmiri language to delectable and piquant Kashmiri cuisine (*wazwan*), from *soigné* and debonair Kashmiri dress to our exquisite and aesthetic handicrafts, from our green *coup de maitre* to our quirky palatial and maestro Chinar (*Maple*), there is allure, beauty and irresistibility in every nook and cranny of the heart of the *Vale*.

The Srinagar Smart City

THE USP OF SRINAGAR

As far *Unique Selling Point* of the wen is adverted to, the paramount and intrinsic trafficking attractions which are apt for flourishing and blossoming our economy and withal making it *compos mentis* are:

1. *Saffron*
2. *Walnut*
3. *Almond*
4. *Apple*
5. *Apricot*
6. *Cherry*
7. *Peach*
8. *Handicrafts*
9. *Tourism*
10. *Kashmiri Cuisine*
11. *Medicinal Herbs*
12. *Chinar*
13. *Oils viz Lavender, Rose Oil*

Further, adventurous and venturesome sports viz *Trekking* and *Swimming* could also be constructive and handy trafficking attractions of the burgh.

THE PECULIARITIES OF AN IDEAL SMART CITY

In the opinion of mine, an ideal and quintessential Smart City should bring forth tranquility, serenity, contentment and equanimity to every single one of its burgess. Forbye hereunder divulged provisions and prerequisites should be bestowed and conferred to single one of its *oppidans* :

1. 24/7 leccy, Wireless Fidelity (*Wi-Fi*), water supply and milk repository via conduits escorted by meters.

2. Subterranean and hypogeal power apparatus and framework with cables, wires and transformers all sub terrestrial.

3. Six lane overriding roadways with filthiness and grime modulating innards plus imperative for every single vehicle proprietor to have pollution checking *mod cons* equipped in his automobile.

4. Use of *e-rickshaws* and bicycles to be invigorated and emboldened.

5. Veto and embargo on vehicles in emporia and public places, and contriving of Parking Complexes to fight shy of gridlock.

6. 30 to 50 deck buildings in the bosom of the *wen* with earth tremor and inundation impervious contrivance and impeccable Surveillance apparatus with cameras, CCTVs to be lodged in every *nook and cranny* of the burgh.

7. A flawless Smart City must be a nerve centre for erudition, education and knowledge.

8. Cleanness should be made *sine qua non* for living with installation of two bin system.

9. The *oppidans* of a quintessential Smart City must be diligent and assiduous *en route* for an ideal milieu.

MAJOR ISSUES AND CHALLENGES IN THE CITY

The major bone of contention to the *wen* is the *conflit armê de Kashmir*. Further, hereunder divulged issues may pose a weighty and grave jeopardy to the Smart City:

1. Tainting and contamination of *Adam's ale*, aerosphere and pandemonium pollution.

2. Earth tremor and inundation susceptible stretch.

3. Domiciliary sewage arising from households with plastic, food

wrappers and other non-biodegradable scrapes which are apt to occlude the sewers to torrent predicament.

4. Abysmal superintendence of gridlock.

SOLUTION 'N' REMEDIES

1. Resort to catalic converters in vehicles viz *CO2ube* and *CO2* transmuter. Forbye, embargo on vehicles in emporia and public places, and contriving of Parking Complexes to fight shy of gridlock.

2. Optimizing use of water and circumvent of hurling of scrapes and sewage in water bodies.

3. Plantation of trees and conifers on roadsides to evade pandemonium pollution.

4. Use of *e-rickshaws*, bicycles and bio-plastics to be invigorated

and emboldened. Withal, veto on non-biodegradable items.

5. Modern and *a la mode* technology to be espoused while lying the substratum of buildings to evade vandalism due to torrents and earth tremors.

6. Sanitizing of sewers at symmetrical interludes to dodge obturating.

AREAS IN THE *WEN* ASKING FOR ATTENTION

The manors and realms to be evolved and vertex precedence turfs in the *wen* which entail colossal scrutiny and precipitate steps for burgeoning and blossoming and withal forging and making them *vie and competent* at sphere level are:

1. *Fatehkadel*
2. *Zonimar*
3. *Old Soura*
4. *Tangpora*
5. *Darwan*
6. *Baghban pora*
7. *Galwan pora*
8. *Badamwari*

In addition to these above divulged areas of the *wen*, some other towns of the old city also require   colossal scrutiny and due attention.

CONCLUSION

Our premier *wen* has already procured renown, stardom and fame in the entire orb and if this exquisite burgh is given a smart footing and repute, the time is not too far when Srinagar would be a facsimile archetypal Smart City for all the urban areas on the sphere.

The Srinagar Smart City

Musharraf Shaheen

The Srinagar Smart City

ABOUT THE AUTHOR

The author who writes under the *pseudonym* **Musharraf Shaheen** is from *the wounded paradise (Kashmir)* and is currently studying in Radiant Public School Anantnag. *Shaheen* writes for local newspapers, print journals and magazines regularly on Kashmir, History, Science, Literature and issues adverting to the Muslims.

The Srinagar Smart City

Musharraf Shaheen

The Srinagar Smart City

Thanks for reading

The Srinagar Smart City

For any sort of propositions whatsoever, please feel free to contact me on the following email id

themajesticshaheen@gmail.com